Hope Crossroads

Hope Gardner

Order this book online at www.trafford.com
or email orders@trafford.com

Most Trafford titles are also available at major online book retailers.

Print information available on the last page.

ISBN: 978-1-4907-7802-0 (sc)
ISBN: 978-1-4907-7804-4 (hc)
ISBN: 978-1-4907-7803-7 (e)

Library of Congress Control Number: 2016917413

Trafford rev.   10/19/2016

www.trafford.com
North America & international
toll-free: 1 888 232 4444 (USA & Canada)
fax: 812 355 4082

Contents

Poem for My Father

My father is Jeffers Walter Gardner.

J.W. for short.

He was born into this world.

World that give you challenges and upside downs.

My father has done lot of things.

Things that amazed me.

Make me proud.

Proud to be his daughter.

Daughter of his five kids.

He is a strong man.

Man that has went through so much.

Much in his young and older life.

He never graduate high school.

See all his children succeed where he did.

He took care of his siblings at a young age.

Learn how to appreciate hard work.

Work to support a family with his bare hands.

Suffer so much loss at an early age with his parents.

Later on, suffer again having to deal with death of his siblings.

He is the last survivor of his siblings.
Watching him trying not to cry hurt me.
He retired his job for his wife to go do what she loves to
help take care of me.
I spent most of my time with my father.
He is a good father.
He is full of spirit, laughter, and greatness.
He loves his children and family.
Love my father.
He is the best.

Poem for My Mother

My mom is great.

Great with her job.

Job dealing with patients dying soon.

She makes them feel better and help them.

She has great stories about her family.

Her family that always seems to have a good time.

She acts like a child with her dancing and trying to make you laugh.

She willing to help her children with anything.

She worries, give advice, and always center of attention.

She has this way with people and people love her.

She also does everything not just for her children for everything one else.

She is not afraid to speak her mind.

She always wants to know what in her children's lives.

She always traveling and nothing slow her down.

Listen to every problem.

Published author twice.

Go to church every Sunday.

·········●···········

One thing she will do for any of her children is defend
them, when someone publicly try to insult them or be very
snippy.
She will say something and people will back off.
Also, learning to love my father from a bunch of letters.
Got marry at an early age.
She has some struggles from going from job to job at an
early age.
Having to learn to live from what you got.
Suffering from loss of her father and mother.
Almost dying from having me be premature baby and I
almost died.
She is a strong and spiritual woman.
That is a great mother to have and as she says she is most
important one of God's child.

Tribute to Larry Shaw

Larry Shaw is my best friend's father.
Father to me too.
He was nice and kind.
Kind soul that touch people's hearts.
Hearts that was sad from his passing.
He makes some jokes.
He tells some stories.
He was an interesting guy.
Guy that I got to know a couple time.
He treated me like I was one of his own children.
He didn't see no skin color when he looks at me.
He welcomes me with open arms
He makes sure I feel at home.
He was so full of life, when I see him with his family.
Family that I consider like my own.
He was so cool and awesome.
You never seem to want to leave their home.
I was so sad to hear the news.

••••••••••●•••••••••

News hurt me like I loss a family member.
I hate to see my best friend suffer like that.
He went to a better place where there is no suffering and
pain.
The place where good people go and watch down on the
living.
I am going to miss him.

My Best Friend

I don't have too many best friends.

Friends seems to drift apart.

Apart from one another.

But, I have one friend.

Friend that I will consider to be my best friend.

Best friend until the day I died.

Her name is Faith.

Faith is like a sister to from another mother.

She is a therapist for free listening to my problem.

My protector from people that give me hard time.

My fashion consultation for suggesting what might look good on me.

She always never forgets my birthday.

She always tries to be there for me, when I need her.

Always one phone call away.

Tell her my hopes and dreams and don't think that stupid.

Will stick by me, when people have abandon me before.

She accepts that we are different and are the same.

Having cool and awesome moments that will stick for centuries.

·············●·············

Will caught me when I have fall.
She will try to cheer me up.
We act totally crazy together.
She is my best friend and I am glad to call her that after all
these years.

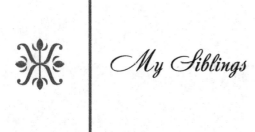

My Siblings

My siblings are way older than me.

They took care of me when I was little.

They were my babysitters basically.

I have two brothers and two sisters.

The two brothers are always smiling.

Smiling like it is permanently on their faces.

They always close and joke around a lot.

They act weird sometimes and I give them a look.

Look where I wonder where is their sanity at.

My sisters love shopping with me.

We love to go in malls and other stores.

Then, we have different opinions of clothes.

Sometimes, I am one side with one sister about this topic or the other way around.

Also, we like trying new things like food.

We go to restaurants and love talking about food like food critics.

My siblings are always there for me, when I need them.

We travel together and cranking up the good times.

Laughing at each other for like some funny moments that
you can even put on television.
We gather for the important moments.
Help each other out.
The most important fact is that we love each other.
That is all that matter doesn't it.

Family Dinners

Dinner is just a specific time you eat.

Eat around the last part of the day.

Day where it is food being prepared.

Prepared by someone.

Someone in your family.

Family that have one or many moments.

Moments to pause out of their busy schedules.

Schedules that occupy your whole days.

Days of being busy with something.

Something special about gathering around.

Around the table with people you love.

Love your entire life.

Life that you shared with them.

Those family members talking about anything.

Anything that can be ranged from work to little things.

Things that can turn into laughter.

Laughter with silly jokes.

Jokes into memories about certain moments.

Moments that you are thankful for.

For having family to share stuff with.

With good food being passed around.
Around watching television together.
Together where sometimes you don't get to see each other
most of the time.
Time where you enjoy company.
Company that make you smile.
Smile that show happiness.
Happiness that we can't take for granted.
This is the meaning of family dinners that we shouldn't
lose and don't take for granted.

People

There is people all over the place.
If you watch closely.
Their whole temperaments show
Show without them realizing it.
It is from the way they dress to the way they walk.
Walking from day to day.
Day just thinking about something.
Something that can go from the blink in the eye.
Or something that wedge in their permanent.
Their facial expressions about certain things.
To the way their talk about things in their accent.
Accents telling where they from originally.
Their whole lives they wear on their sleeves.
Some can hide it well like a magician doing a magic trick.
Some just express way too much.
Come in all different color, shapes, and sizes.
Just set in different environments.
Environments control by the universe or science.
Interacting with each other.

···········●···········

How we as a people can grow or shrink in a situation.
Situation that can test people in millions of ways.
This is a true definition of people that you will never find
in a book, just a feeling.

Social Issues

Social issues that will always happen.
Happen within our society.
Society that has these rules.
Rules about everything.
Everything to exclude people.
People that don't fit.
Fit into a perfect box.
Box on how society scare.
Scared of people of different color, orientation, and
idealism.
Scared of them being better and succeeding.
Succeeding into having better ideas, work, or anything.
Anything that make them look like a person.
Society treated them like dirt.
Dirt that can't be deal with.
Just look in such distain that come up with names.
Names that mean to hurt.
But, they take in pride.

Stand up what they believe and laugh society in the faces.
We can solve these problems without hate and violence.
With love, compassion, and understanding.
Understanding by getting the story out there.
There for people to talk about.
So, social issues can be cut down.
Down by years and have peace.
Social issues happen every day.
Days where we need to have a conservation.
Instead, ignoring it by pushing underneath the rug.

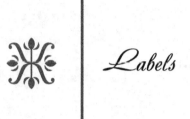 *Labels*

Labels is something to put on
On to know where they belong or what it is.
Now, labels are symbols.
Symbols for people.
People that are different.
Different and unique.
Unique where people don't understand.
Understand to be in their shoes.
Use to shame someone.
To put someone down.
To make them belittle.
To act like someone's trash.
But, the haters got fool.
Fool by those people.
People that take those labels.
Labels with pride and strut around.
Around not caring about what those haters think.
They are just tearing those labels up.
Just living life and being happy.

·············●·············

Happy that doing whatever they want without being scared.

Fighting back with them looking back.

Back with their middle finger in the air to the haters.

Haters are getting scared themselves.

Haters' power is getting weak and their voices are getting block.

Can't control hard work of good people that don't need labels.

Labels for someone unique, not different color or orientation for bullying.

No labels anymore. People are just people.

Body Shaming

People try to love their bodies
Their bodies have imperfects.
Imperfects and curves.
Curves that are part of them
Looking at themselves.
Finding every single thing wrong with them
Different than what people they love see.
Seeing their shelves as hideous and fat.
Fat that will never go away.
Try to make these thoughts go away.
They are being remind by their peer and media.
Media telling them that will never be this perfect image.
Image that people adored.
Having people worship at their feet.
That only certain people talk to.
Will never put off certain good looking clothes.
Clothes only for the skinny and glamorous.
No one will find them attracted.
Put them down with words and images.
Making them beat myself every day.

·············●·············

Looking at food with hate instead enjoying.
Bitter with jealously with others that have to compete.
Crying out for help.
Thanks media and society for putting this negative
feedback on just ordinary plain people.
We now need for your approval to feel beautiful about
ourselves.

Life Lessons

Seem like there is a classroom.

Classroom that you will be your whole life.

Your subjects vary.

Vary by different experiences in life.

You are going to have tests, assignments, and review.

Review what is going on so far.

You are going to have to keep learning.

Learning by teachers.

Teachers are the people that has most impact.

Impact where you take something out on it.

You probably won't pass the first time.

Going to get held back couple of times.

Up until you pass that particular lesson.

Some lessons are easier.

Some lessons are harder and you struggle.

Struggle with an issue in your life and have to overcome it.

You keep graduating from this classroom.

You will never get out of this classroom.

Life lessons is reality.

Reality that you are always facing.

Rejection

Rejection is like a poison.
Poison slowly steeping in.
In my head.
Head full with doubts.
Doubts and insecurities.
Insecurities that broke me into pieces.
Pieces that turn into tears.
Tears stinging in my eyes.
Eyes soon done with the tears.
Tears that dried up into anger.
Anger at myself.
Myself for never being good enough.
Enough for the world.
World that helping me build back up.
Up to give me some thicker skin.
Skin to make me try again.
Again until I get what I want.
I want is for someone to say yes.

Memories

Memories are like a strip of film.
Each of these film strips contains something.
Something important.
Important that happens in your life.
Life consist of small details.
Details like your firsts.
First of everything.
Everything you accomplished.
Accomplish every single day.
Days that can be filled with joy.
Joy, sadness, and struggles.
Struggles that plagues us sometimes.
Sometimes, certain memories we picked.
Picked out of billions.
Billions we play back like a video in our minds.
Mind that has the remote control.
Control to rewind, forward, pause, and play.
Play a memory to remind ourselves.

·········●··········

Ourselves to do something differently.

Can be cautionary tale.

The tale of anything.

Any memories are parts of an epic movie of a lifetime.

Battle of The Lovers

There is a battlefield.
Battlefield stood two people.
People on opposite sides.
Sides were both think they are right.
Right on their view.
View of the battle of the relationship.
Relationship where this start.
Start with it being sweet and innocent.
Innocent turn into disaster.
Disaster with lies and demands.
Demands turn into arguments.
Arguments turn into hate.
Hate fuels the weapons.
Weapons in their hands.
Hands ready to fight.
Fighting until someone bleeds.
Bleeds with every cuts.
Cuts that are deep
Deep in blood over the ground.

Ground that buried your relationship.
Relationship that is over.
Over time both sides heal.
Heal but distance.
Kind of friends.
Never will be close as they were.
This is the Battle of the Lovers.

Surviving Retail

Retail is a job.

Job that will test your patience.

Patience with no consistent schedule.

Schedule have to give up most Saturdays.

Saturdays where it supposed to be fun.

Fun will be one of those weird days.

Days you don't expect to have off.

Off to work to punch in.

Punch in to put a smile.

Smile until your face hurt.

Hurt where you start to believe.

Believe you not just in it for money.

Money to deal with customers.

Customers of all types.

Types that can range from.

From talking to you like la therapist.

Therapist to punching bag packing a punch.

Punch to annoying things.

Things that reminds them of you.

You dealing with drama.

* * * * * * * * * * ● * * * * * * * * * * *

Drama with coworkers.
Coworkers with cliques.
Clique that are in high school, where popular take the
credit and the losers do the hard work.
Just to work to make a paycheck.
Paycheck to survive in today's world.
World of surviving retail.

Phoenix

The phoenix is not just some mystical bird on fire.

It is a symbol.

Symbol of starting over.

Starting over from the past.

The past that stand before me.

Me with all the pieces from emotions

Emotions that was full of anger, jealously, and turmoil.

Turmoil that seems to been beyond repair.

Repair by the burning.

Burning of these pieces that damage myself.

Myself in glorious fire getting turn into ashes.

Ashes that have a speck of hope.

Hope inside of these ashes.

Ashes that looks so charred.

Charred slowly began to come together.

Together into a whole new person.

Person that is better than before.

Before I was weak and fragile.
Fragile by hardships.
Hardships that beat me down.
Down where I can rise up.
Up to be reborn.
I am the phoenix.

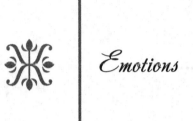

Emotions

Emotions are that can't be explained.

Explained by a clear definition.

Definition of what is a part of you.

You are experience every day.

Days, years, and lifetime.

Lifetime going from one emotion to the next one.

One that can happen almost very second.

Second that can be cause by anything.

Anything that can happen to you.

You just react to that situation.

Situation that can go so many ways.

Ways to deal with that with a certain emotion.

Emotions are many different things.

Things that can be express with your eyes or face.

Face can say one thing but something deep inside is
different.

Different with complications.

Complications things that we will never understand.

Understand that we accept it.

It is just a part of everyday living.

·········●··········

Living with these emotions that can't always be explained
by science.
Science can't explain why people do what they do from
their emotions.
Emotions that can be turn off depending on the type of
person.
Person that can be human or a monster.
Emotions is what make people who they are and how they
react.
But, these complicated things of life what makes us human.

Anger

Anger is one of those dangerous emotion.
Emotion that can end very badly.
Badly where someone can get hurt.
Hurt someone or yourself.
Yourself trying to bottle it down.
Down with inside you.
You want to do something.
Something that is boiling.
Boiling like a volcano.
Volcano that will erupt.
Erupt with lava creeping down.
Down the sides burning.
Burning until it reaches its destination.
Destination for destruction.
Destruction to wanting something to happen.
Happen where you want to scream.
Scream out and punch something.

Something that crumble.

Crumble to make the other people want to cry.

Cry to get someone to feel that pain.

Anger is hard to control.

Control is the key to anger.

To deal with the little ticks of anger every day.

Days

Periods of time.
Time where things are set in 24 hours.
Hours that goes into midnight.
Midnight to another.
Another day.
Days are things.
Things that appear on calendars.
Keeping up for appointments, school, or work.
Work in mysterious ways.
Ways that happen every single second.
Second where you make a decision.
Decision that can affect.
Affect certain things.
Things like the everyday stuff.
Stuff where it could be something different.

Different days that are just passing the time.

Time where people are doing everything.

Everything that keep us occupied.

Occupied with situations.

Situations where it just minor or serious.

Serious where we think.

Think about anything.

Days are just one of the many things in the universe that keep us going from telling time or just making us do things that is a part of life.

The Past

The past is the most powerful thing.
Thing where is a point.
Point of time.
Time of someone's history.
History that can shape you.
You as a person.
Person learning from mistakes.
Mistakes or painful experiences.
Experiences keep you in chains.
Chains wrapping.
Wrapping around you so tight.
Tight that you need to bust out.
Out of the sorrow, anger, and pain.
Pain that sometimes keep you from happiness.
Happiness that you strived for.
For where you learn to grow.
Grow into this beautiful person.
Person that become stronger.
Stronger from their past.
Past where it is a learning curve for everyone.

 *Fear*

Fear is an emotion.

Emotion that can cripple.

Cripple your senses.

Senses where you stop thinking.

Thinking of just feeling.

Feeling paralyze where you stand.

Standing there just wanting.

Wanting to throw up.

Up and run away.

Away of whatever scare you.

You can overcome.

Overcome fear by steps.

Steps where it starts out slowly.

Slowly, fear is starting to disappear.

Disappear, until it stat not having control of you.

You have control of your fear.

Fear is nothing, but a defense.

Defense of something new and scary.

That is fear.

Tears

Sitting alone.
Alone in a room.
Room where there is nothing.
Nothing, but me.
Me with my head down.
Down with my hands.
Hands covering my eyes.
Eyes starting to water.
Water that let out a single tear.
Tear coming down.
Down one by one.
One on the floor.
Floor start to get wet.
Wet starts slowly become.
Becoming a puddle.
Puddle is now a pool.
Pool of tears.
Tears full of anger and sadness.
Sadness filling up the room.

·············●·············

Room full of tears.
Tears drowning me.
I am being dragged down.
Down to the bottom.
Bottom where I float unconscious.
Unconscious in tears.

Prayers

Prayers are spiritual.
Spiritual beliefs.
Beliefs for any religion.
Religions searching for answers.
Answers for their questions.
Questions about the world.
World that has become cruel.
Cruel enough where people are crying for help.
Help with their pain, struggles, and wishes.
Wishing for something to make it better.
Better to comfort them in a time, where there is no hope
in this world.

 # Journey

Journey is something profound.
Profound by challenges.
Challenges in life.
Life of you.
You surround by events.
Events that shape you.
You are walking down a road.
Road that has bumps and turns.
Turns that questions you.
You are making decisions.
Decisions by emotions.
Emotions can make us rise.
Rise up and continue on our way.
Way to a fulfill life.
Life full of happy.
Happy within ourselves.
The journey is a spiritual metaphor for the road of finally
be satisfied in your life.

Losers

People that loses are the ones that get pick last.
Last for everything.
Everything that has to deal with winning something.
Something that matters to them.
They are always coming last place.
Place where they don't get recognized.
Recognized for trying.
Trying with the fabric of their being.
Being more pessimistic than optimistic.
Optimistic where they faked it.
It knowing where they can be more realistic.
Realistic to situations where they self-doubt.
Doubt they can get anything.
Anything where they see the winners lifting that trophy.
Trophy where you can see.
See with bitter and jealousy.
Jealousy that burns into the body.
Body and mind on the same page for once.

Once or forever stop trying.

Trying their best.

Best of giving their all.

All of the hard work.

Work where stop pleasing people.

People they became harden.

Harden by experiences.

Experiences that they don't see in rose covered glasses.

Glasses of the truth and became stronger. They are the
losers of the end of spectrum.

 *Favorites*

Everyone has their favorites.

Favorites food, music, or anything.

Anything they like.

But, there is a different types of favorites.

Favorites that can exclude a person.

Person that don't get the same type of privileges.

Privileges like the favorites.

Favorites can get what they want without trying.

Trying to be buddies with someone important.

Important where they overlook the other people.

People might deserve more.

More than some excuses.

Excuses that are makeup of top of their head.

Head where they can just lie to you.

You just accept with a nod and a fake smile.

Smile that hid the frustrations of this ridiculous method.

Methods to tell someone they are not good enough for them.

Favorites can get away with things.

Things you can't.

Make the same things, but yours is never exciting.

Exciting to be treated with the same respect.

Respect as those that are treated like kings and queens.

Favorites is one of those things you have to deal with and going to learn to not care anymore.

 *Home*

Home is where you live in.

It is not just a house to support your head.

It can be anywhere.

Anywhere that is your own.

Own where you feel safe and love.

Love the atmosphere where you want to bath in it.

Where you can make memories.

Memories of happiness and light.

Light full of laughter and warmth.

Warmth full of friends and family.

Family time that is cherish every second in a day.

Day where you relax from a long day of work.

Home is where you feel the most comfort.

Comfort from the storms that passing your way.

Way that try to tear you down or destroy you.

You spend most of your time there.

There where you just can get away from everything.

Everything that is distracting and problematic.

Home is what is in your heart and where you feel the safest.

That is the true meaning of home.

Pressure

Pressure is a trigger.

Trigger that can happen anytime.

Anytime and anywhere.

Anywhere that have an intense situation.

Situation where your head is spinning.

Spinning around and around.

Around then your feet feel like running.

Running to the nearest corner.

Corner where people are stressing you.

You putting your hands on your head.

Head like a headache that never stopped.

Never stop with the constant time constraints.

Constraints where a whole lists of problems.

Problems that start flooding in.

In where that are beating so hard.

Hard where you just want to scream.

Scream to stop.

Stop time where everything frozen still.

Still, to turn back time to have more time.

Time to do everything.

Everything that need your constant attention.

Pressure can make you crumble and you have to face like a warrior.

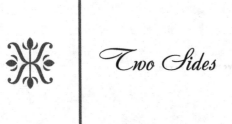 *Two Sides*

There is me standing in one corner.
In another corner, there is another person.
Person looks just like me.
I am wearing white.
The another me is wearing black.
We look at each other across the ring.
Looking at each other with distain.
Distain for each other.
We slowing coming from our corners.
We heard the bell.
We start to fight.
Fight like our lives are depending on it.
Fighting until one of us is the winner.
Winner can be me with all the good.

······●·······

Or it could be me with all the bad.
Sometimes, this fight can turn into many rounds.
Rounds that will last forever.
Forever in time, when I make a decision.
Decision that can feel right at the time.
Time where my bad side love to come out.
Out to beat me to get her way.
Sometimes, I could be the winner.
Winner that make me not feel guilty or regret.
Regret for the rest of my life.
Make me feel happy.
Sometimes, my bad side wins.
Wins, when I get so fed up that I go on attack.
This fight will always remain inside me and inside you too.

Sunset

Sunset is one of the most appreciate thing in this world.
World that is coming undone.
Undone where the problems will never be solved.
Sunset is perfect setting.
Setting where it balances of sun.
Sun that represent the day.
Day that is slowly become night.
It has set of colors.
Colors that has bright and darkness in it.
It reminds me of what people go through.
Through every day in their life.
Life full of thoughts.
Thoughts of what how that day effect you.
A lasting of reminder of the lasting day.
Day could range from happy to angry.
Sunset are the universe creation.
Creation where poets and philosophers write about it.
Or where artist painted it when inspiration hit.
Sunset means so much more to people than just a thing.
It is something where you look and reflect and just
beautiful at the same time.

Lies

Lies are little stories.

Stories of piece of fiction.

Fiction that you come up with.

With on top of your head.

Head where you know what can be believable.

Believable where people can take your word for.

For where they can't question.

Question the trust they put in you.

You have different types of lies.

Lies where you don't want to be caught.

Caught doing something appalling.

Appalling where they would look in disgust.

Disgust at what you did.

There is the other type of lie where you consider.

Consider of someone's feeling.

Feeling you don't want to see their disappointment in the face.

So, you tell a lie to please them.

The other type is just don't want to do anything.

Anything involve something for someone else.

You just want to be leave alone or feeling selfish that day.

·············●·············

Just be convince for you.

Lies can have huge consequences or don't effect in anyone.

Just be careful when you lie.

It can catch up to you.

You don't know what truth and lies yourself.

Temptation

Temptation is one of those dangerous things.

Things that is become very powerful.

Powerful to resist.

Resist with the will power.

Power that is inside you.

You have choices that is so tempting.

Tempting with some bad choices.

Choices that seem so easy at first.

First, where it benefits you.

You want to have it all.

All without being patience.

Patience and goodness.

Goodness that is a part of you.

You want to that dark part.

Part that don't care about any rules.

Rules or restraints in life.

Life where it can make it so hard.

Hard to do the good thing.

Thing where you want to feel better.

Better without the moral compass.

Compass of desires, backstabbing, and wishes.

Wishes that can destroy yourself and someone else.

Temptation is those thing to overcome and be tested every day.

Babies

Babies are born.
Born into the world.
World that seems to be brand new to them.
With their little hands and eyes.
Eyes observing everything around them.
They are so simple creations.
Creations that know what they want.
Having so simple emotions.
Emotions that don't deal too deep yet.
Just switch to one emotion to the next.
They are always playing.
Playing and don't have to worry about bills.
Can be taught very easily.

Easily where their being can be who they are in years.
They have adorable faces.
Faces that don't care about looks just yet.
They have no care in the world.
They are just so fascinating.
Learning how to crawl, walk, and talk.
Something that come from two people.
Babies make us think it would be nice.
Nice to not having to know the complicated things about
yourself and the world.

Role Models

Role Models are people.
People that other people look up to.
To somehow guide them or be them.
Role Models can be anyone.
Anyone that seem to impact your life.
They seem to have to set standards.
Standards that are good and doing no wrong.
Wrong like something very sinful.
Sinful that will shock society.
They have to watch their steps.
Steps that other people look for.
For there are all types of role models.
Role Models that save life.
Life that have full of potential.

They are fighting for human rights.

Doing what best for the greater good.

Other types of role models are we worship.

Worship from some media or celebrity like state.

They make mistakes with expect them like they should set example for younger people.

The best role model would have to be yourself.

It is the person that can do the things you want to and set their own example.

Role Models are different people and just got to look.

Changes

Changes are always happening.
Happening whether you like it or not.
Not in your regular routine.
Routine that you got used to.
To make your life make sense.
Sense where you feel comfortable.
Comfortable and safe where there is no risk.
Risk of not knowing.
Knowing that is unavoidable.
Unavoidable where you got to face it.
It is to a point where you have to learn.
Learn to try to adapt.
Adapt and fit it to your routine.
Routines to more drastic things.

Things that changes you in different ways.

Ways that can affect you emotional and physical.

Physical where people notice.

Notice there is something about you.

You can have an aura.

Aura where it can just be emotional.

Emotional that can affect the outside.

Outside where you can feet something different.

Changes are all different types and can happen in time.

Time where changes will always be a part of you and learn

how to adapt to these once in a while.

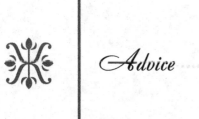 *Advice*

Advice is some words.

Words of guidance.

Guidance of someone.

Someone that trying to understand the situation.

Situation that you have no solution to.

To the problem that is so complex.

Complex where you need to get another person's
perspective.

Perspective where it can be a whole different insight.

Insight where it can fix what have baffled you.

You can take the advice from the other person.

Person can give all sort of advice.

Advice that can help you.

You can be happy with the outcome.

Outcome where there is a person that can give you bad
advice.

Advice where you got to watch out.

Out for the consequences up ahead.

Ahead, where there is the final type of advice.

Advice where the other people love hearing themselves.

They are the ones that want to be the first one.

One to give this wisdom.

Wisdom that love talking about themselves.

Or just love to receive thanks.

Thanks that can go in their heads.

Heads where they are attention seeking people.

Advice can be a good thing. Just have to find the right person to be there and listen. Giving sound advice and willing to help you. Not just themselves.

 *Souls*

Souls are something inside you.
You can't see it physically.
Physically, but it is spiritual.
Spiritual and mystical.
Mystical of what we are.
We are as people.
People try to explain.
Explain how so many emotions can affect you.
You in every decisions and in moments.
Moments where you can make impact.
Impact of where you can be anything that you can live
with.
With all that can determine.
Determine if you are just a good person.
Person that has flaws, but still do a good thing.
Thing that can be a bad person.

Person that don't care.

Care and thinks there are no flaws.

Flaws that is show and disgusting.

Disgusting like a monster.

Monster that think it is they are in the right.

Right where it is wrong.

But, there is can be a changes in souls.

These changes can decide where the souls go.

Go into whatever places that can rewarded or punishes us.

Us as living or dying.

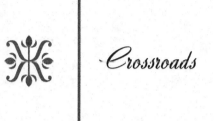 *Crossroads*

There have been many crossroads in my life.
Life that can be really difficult sometimes.
Sometimes, where the answers can be really clear.
Clear as day.
Day where I can deal with anything.
Anything that life can throw at me.
Me where I conquer something.
Something great.
Great things sometimes become worst.
Worst things that has me in circles.
Circles that lead me into a repeat.
Repeat until I want to give up.
Give up on the path.
Path that come from my decisions.
Decisions to do something.
Something along the way.
Ways that will cross my path all the time.
Time of every second of every day.
Day where I have to overcome to get to the next chapter.
Chapter of my life.
Life for me is full of crossroads.

Broken

I use to be so strong.
Strong at the beginning.
Beginning where I was naïve.
Naïve where I thought I was invincible.
Invincible to how the universe works.
Works in its cruel way staring back at me.
Me just standing there be happy.
Happy of anything can't hurt me.
Me later on find out.
Out where the universe will punish me.
Me soon or later.
Later, people with their cruel words.
Words that stings.
Stings to the core.
Core until their actions speak louder.
Louder where I start getting in my head.
Head full of negative thoughts.

Thoughts of myself.

Myself start to crumble slowly.

Slowly shattering into pieces.

Pieces of glass.

Glass across the floor.

Floor where all of the positive things went too.

Feeling like always doubting myself.

Myself as worthless.

Worthless to the world.

World that has broken me into pieces.

Pieces that need to be unbroken.

College

College is not just a school institution.
Institution of farther education.
Education where anyone can go.
Go if they are young or old.
Old where you not a teenage anymore.
More where you can take classes.
Classes that interest you.
You can get to be happy.
Happy to have something to get up.
Up out of bed.
Bed where you want to work.
Work where it is not just a place.
Place where you can make money.
Money that can't fill that hole in your heart.

Heart where college can give you that.

That can work with you.

You and your situations.

Situations that life has already in stored.

Stored where you learn something.

Something that you can take.

Take into life and use.

Use to your advantage.

Advantage of having something fulfilled.

Fulfilled with joy.

College means this.

Gossip

It starts as nothing.
Nothing turns into something.
Something small.
Small whispers.
Whispers of words.
Words of half-truths.
Truths of someone.
Someone that gains interest.
Interest of people involve.
Involve with a matter.
Matter of somewhat news.
News that cause drama.
Drama turns into jealousy.
Jealousy that give attention.
Attention that people always love.
Love to heard.

Heard about what happens.

Happens cause sides to take place.

Place where people are against each other.

Other where it can cause cliques.

Gossip is a game you have to learn very well to survive or

get stepped on.

Loyalty

Loyalty happens over trust.

Trust where you can confide in each other.

Other with things no one know about.

About friendship and doing anything.

Anything for that person.

Person that will have your back.

Back full of support.

Support against those who don't get you.

You build a bond.

Bond that is earn over time.

Time where it is tested.

Tested against number of things.

Things that required loyalty.

Loyalty where you need in life.

Life where there is all sort of enemies.

Enemies that are putting you down.

Down where you can never get up again.

Again, loyalty is defined in many ways.

Ways of friendship, family, and people.

People that have been there for you.

You at your worst possible moments.

Moments where you realize loyalty is all around you.

You just have to do trial and error all the time.

Time where you need to know who is good or bad for you.

Loyalty is everything in life.

 *Hypocrite*

There is always a person.
Person that like to point finger.
Finger to judge.
Judging someone's actions.
Actions like they are God themselves.
Themselves thinking they have good virtues.
Virtues showing the world they are saints.
Saints they are not.
Not what they portrayal.
Portrayal in front of the whole world.
World that is full of gray.
Gray of mistakes and choices.
Choices to make people feel worst.
They are everywhere.

Everywhere and every time you look around.

Around and need to look inside you own heart.

Heart that is also can have crazy morals.

Morals that can make you look better too.

But, they are probably doing the same thing.

Thing that they are afraid to face.

Face choices and decisions that they don't want to admit.

The truth is and always will be that everyone is a hypocrite.

If they want to be or not

It is just the way it works.

I Am Woman

I am a woman.
Woman that suppose to look weak.
Weak and helpless toward men.
Men thinking, I should act.
Act more like a lady.
Lady that supposed to wear dresses.
Dresses that look nice.
Nice and conservative.
Conservative and having kids.
Kids that I am not ready.
Ready or don't want.
Want me to cook and clean.
Clean, but I love being messy.
Messy and sometimes underrated.
Underrated by my worth.
Worth that come from ideas and hard work.

Work that I get no respect.

Respect and just look over.

Over and suppose to be make a man happy.

Happy for them, but unhappiness for me.

Me just breaking out of the stereotype woman.

Woman that they still want, but modern times got rid of.

Of the cooks and good babysitters of men.

Men that want me to drop everything for them.

Them becoming whiny and needy.

Needy like I am their mother.

Mother I am not.

I am a strong willed woman taking no prisoners and be
independent. I am woman. Deal with it.

Apologies

Apologies are regrets.

Regrets of something.

Something you did that was offence.

Offence for someone else.

Someone that might not deserve it.

But, there are the easy apologies.

The ones that are not showing up or an accident of sort.

Sort of apologies that is no big deal.

Deal with the other apologies.

Apologies that take time to forgive.

Forgive what you did out of anger.

Anger, resentment, or jealousy.

These ones can't take just two small words and everything
is forgotten.

Forgotten what big mess you make.
Make out of chaos.
Chaos that hurt.
Hurt that other person.
Person that will feel that.
That and will always remember whatever you did.
Sometimes, you will never get forgiven.
Sometimes, you will have to face the guilt and deal.
Apologies comes in different ways.
It is just what situation you are in.
Will it be forgotten and forgiven or will it be never?

 *Revenge*

Revenge is a tempting thing.

Thing that seems so good.

Good, but so dangerous.

Dangerous on how far you are willing to go.

Go where you have to live with it.

It within your soul.

Soul that is where your heart is at.

At where the emotions are.

Are the deciding factors of who you are?

Are you capable?

Capable to see someone hurt.

Hurt so much.

Much where you like to see them in pain.

Pain and suffering to make you happy.

Happy to get them back.

Back where you are smiling.

Smiling while they are self-destructing.

Destructing into pieces.

Pieces where they can't get back up.

Up from the damage.

Damage and chaos you put upon them.

Revenge is one of those test.

Test where it will decide are you a good or bad person.

Person that have remorse or not.

Flirting

Flirting is a game.

Game starts out with one person.

Person that shows interest.

Interest in another person.

Person that is attractive.

Attractive that catch their eye.

Eye that has a little tinkle.

Tinkle that know what to do.

Do is play a little game.

Game that has many tricks.

Tricks to capture the other's attention.

Attention with little gestures.

Gestures like hair flips, looks, and conservations.

Conservations that are playful.

Playful with laughter.

Laughter then some type of lines.

Lines that make them want to play the game.

Game turn into two.

Two people start to like this game.

Game where it not too seriously.

Flirting can lead to something or not.

But, the game of flirting is fun.

One of the fun part of life.

The World

The world is full of people.
People all around.
Around doing different things.
Things people do every day.
Every day that do seem the normal.
Normal thing we don't think about.
About history that make the world what it is.
The battles and triumphs that some people make.
Make for our lives to become better.
Better to survive and to live in this world.
World where we did take steps forward.
Forward with our way of thinking and acceptance.
Acceptance that took so long to get.

But, we took steps back.

Back with the hate and judgments.

Judgments of how the world should be perfect.

Perfect for some people.

People that need to look down in their hearts.

Hearts that need to start caring.

Caring and we can take steps forward.

Forward to the utopia that we all wish.

Wish they could happen.

Utopia is peace.

Peace need to be in the world.

The world needs this more than ever before.

Hope

Hope is something positive.
Positive to believe in.
Believe in wanting.
Wanting something to happen.
Happen to be true.
True for something good.
Good coming to chance.
Chance that it will come.
Come to make you happy.
Happiness that can overcome.
Overcome those dark days.
Days that are hard to get out of bed for.
For those days to become brighter.
Brighter with hope.

Hope of a feeling.

Feeling of miracles.

Miracles that don't happen every day.

Day where we need some fulfillment.

Fulfillment from the negativity of the world.

World that we live in.

In where lot of things that can bring us down.

Down with sadness.

Hope is believing for the believers that knows their day
will get better, because of it.

 *Pain*

There are many forms.
Forms that is just physically.
Physically where it just need to be heal.
Heal with some plain old medicine.
Medicine that make you feel better.
Another one is the most common.
Common where someone get on your nerves.
Nerves that why you have to put up with this person.
Person where you have to deal with.
With every single day and want to get away from.
But, the last form of pain is the hardest one.
One where it is hard to get help.
Help that need to come from within.
Within your soul and mind.
Mind full of emotional pain.
Pain that can be a result.

Result of hurt and sadness.

Sadness of some situation.

Situation that you look back on again and again.

Again in your mind thinking you are not good enough.

Enough for this world or it is your fault.

Fault for something and it is not your fault.

It can torture you into shreds.

Shreds into nothingness.

Nothingness where there is a huge ache.

Ache of needing help.

Help that is crying out so loud.

Loud where you just want to be heard. Pain can be stop,

but there are different approaches.

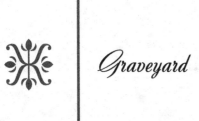

Graveyard

Graveyard are where they buried someone.
Someone that live their life.
Life that is full of memories.
Memories and moments important to them.
Them just wasting away below the ground.
Ground full of dirt.
Dirt that is covered the casket.
Casket among other caskets.
Caskets all over the graveyard.
Graveyard that has seem so haunting.
Haunting with the tombstones.
Tombstones of the people that died.
Died with stories.

Stories that somehow fascinate the living.
Living need to know how they died.
The graveyard seems to be mysterious at night.
Night where the unknown love to come out and play.
Play like there are ghosts coming.
Coming to react or reminding us.
Us to remember the person that have died.
Died and also remembering to live life to the moment.
Moment where you can be scare to died.
Dying is what graveyards remind us of all of that.

Darkness

Darkness is very easy to have.

Have to take certain events.

Events that can cause the darkness.

Darkness where It can come from pain.

Pain, anger, jealousy, and sadness.

It can be just from one.

One to all of them combine.

Combine where it can suck all of the light.

Light that hold the goodness.

Goodness and positivity.

Positivity of rainbows.

Rainbows of happiness.

But, the darkness can come out a little bit.

Bit with the negative thoughts.

Thoughts that can be powerful.

Powerful where you sit in a corner.

•••••••••●•••••••••

Corner looking up and walking toward something.
Something that resemble a funhouse.
Funhouse full of mirrors.
Mirrors that shows you.
You from different perspective.
Perspective where you need the darkness.
Darkness where it only a little bit.
Bit from being too native and be caution.
Caution with other people.
Darkness can help you survive.
Survive anything.
Darkness is not a bad thing. Don't let it grow or you can
become a monster.

Writing

There is a piece of paper.

Paper that is on a desk.

A hand holding a pencil.

Pencil that is sharpen.

Sharpen to be ready.

Ready to be written.

Written on the paper.

Paper is the blank canvas.

Canvas where your imagination is ready.

Ready to be capture.

Capture on the page.

Page that is descriptive.

Descriptive of something that need to be told.

Told in a story.

Story through someone else's eyes.

Eyes where it can take you to places.

Places away from reality.

Reality of life.

Life that is kind of boring at the moment.

Moment where you need excitement.

Excitement that can be capture from writing.

Writing where characters come to life and need to be told.

Told in feelings and expressions.

Writing can do that for people, but most certainly for me.

Writing help me with anything.

Printed in the United States
By Bookmasters